W9-BEC-803

WANYANA AND
MATCHMAKER FROG

Sserukama mayute: olunyiga ku lirye ng' akaaba.
Be kind to me and I will be kind to you.
                                        A Bagandan proverb

For Elizabeth and Charlie
  —M. L.

For Tod Lemkuhl, Toad & Matchmaker
  —C. R.

Wanyana and Matchmaker Frog is based on "The Story of the Frog," from *The Flame Tree and Other Folk-Lore Stories from Uganda,* by Mrs. George (Rosetta) Baskerville. London: Church Missionary Society, 1922.

This story is from the Baganda of Uganda.

© 1998 The Rourke Press, Inc.

ILLUSTRATIONS © Charles Reasoner

Library of Congress Cataloging-in-Publication Data

Lilly, Melinda.
   Wanyana and matchmaker frog: [a Bagandan tale] / retold by Melinda Lilly; illustrated by Charles Reasoner.
      p. cm. — (African tales and myths)
   Summary: A frog repays Wanyana's kindness by helping her pick the right man to be her husband.
   ISBN 1-57103-247-9
   [1. Ganda (African people)—Folklore. 2. Folklore—Uganda.]
I. Reasoner, Charles, ill. II. Title III. Series: Lilly, Melinda. African tales and myths.
PZ8.1.L468Wan 1998
[398.2'089'963957]—dc21   98–23123
                                                                    CIP
                                                                    AC

Printed in the USA

African Tales and Myths

WANYANA

AND MATCHMAKER FROG

A BAGANDAN TALE

Retold by
Melinda Lilly

Illustrated by
Charles Reasoner

The Rourke Press, Inc.
Vero Beach, Florida 32964

Wanyana waved good-bye to her aunties and left the clatter and laughter of the open-air marketplace as it closed for the day. She stepped in time with the jingling of the five cowrie shells she'd received as payment for her bananas.

"Kata-myaboosi, day is much too hot!" she sang to herself as she headed up the hill toward the home she shared with her mother. Soon the cooling dumbi rains of autumn would begin, but not soon enough for Wanyana. She was looking forward to cooling her dusty feet in the pond behind her house when she heard a small voice nearby.

"Help!" it croaked. "Help!"

Wanyana stopped and looked around her. The only movement came from the leaves of banana trees swaying in the muggy breeze. "Where are you?" she called.

"Here on the path," the voice rasped. "Look down."

5

Bending down, Wanyana was astonished to find a tiny frog crusted with dirt. "You? You can talk?" she gasped, staring in wonder at the little creature as she scooped him into her palm.

"I need water," Frog panted. "Please."

"Poor Brother Ndizaala, Little Frog," she said, shading him. "I'll help you." She ran along the trail and through the banana grove, then set him gently in her pond. Wanyana dipped her feet in the shallow water and watched as Frog wallowed contentedly.

"Aahh!" Both she and Frog sighed with pleasure.

After Frog had bathed the mud off his shiny striped skin he paddled over and hopped on top of one of Wanyana's feet. Bowing deeply, he solemnly ribbited, "My name is Yokana. Thank you for saving my life. I will always be your friend and I will repay your kindness someday, gentle woman."

"Woman?" Wanyana smiled. "No, no, I'm still a girl. But soon, I hope." She picked up the tiny frog. "My name is Wanyana," she said, "and I'm happy to be your friend."

Soon shadows cooled the banana grove, signaling that it was time for Wanyana to return home for dinner. She reluctantly said good-bye and went to her hut serenaded by Frog's twilight song.

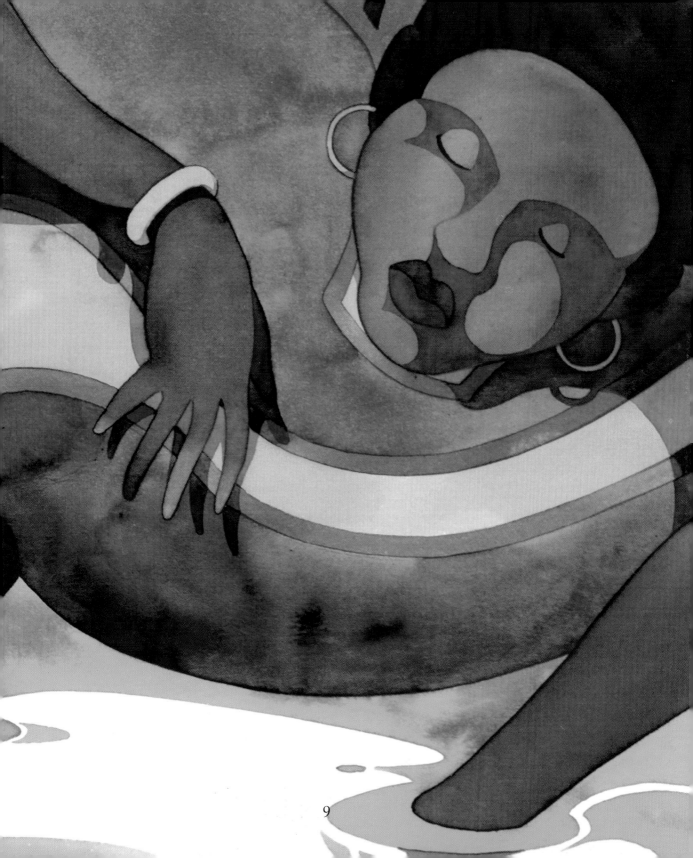

"Mama, you'll never believe what happened. I met a talking frog!" blurted Wanyana as she joined her mother beside the hearth. She dropped the cowrie shells in her mother's palm, adding, "He's in our pond."

"Your aunties and I were right then," said Mama wistfully as she patted Wanyana's tightly curled hair. "Frogs are the guiding spirits of love, my daughter. You're ready to be a bride, ready to start your family. Tomorrow you'll meet and choose your husband from three men your aunties and I have selected for you."

"So soon?" asked Wanyana.

"Do you remember what Sky God promised his daughter and our ancestor Kintu when they were married?" asked Mama, holding Wanyana at arm's length and looking into her eyes.

"That the Baganda people would never die," Wanyana answered.

"Yes, because men and women marry and have children. We Baganda live forever through our children and our children's children. This is a time of joy, Wanyana. You'll see," Mama said.

"All right," Wanyana agreed with a curious smile. "If you and Sky God say so."

Mama put her arm around her daughter. "Tomorrow you'll meet Bwoya of the Honey Bird Clan, Lutaya of the Elephant Clan, and Sempa of the Monkey Clan."

"Do you know them?" asked Wanyana.

"I know their families and their families are good people," said Mama, adding, "If you know the tree, you know the seed."

Wanyana arose at dawn the next morning, unable to stay in bed a moment longer. Her mind whirled, wondering what the day and her future would bring. After a hastily eaten breakfast, she went to the pond.

"Yokana, my friend," she called, looking for him at the water's edge. "I need your help."

Frog hopped out of the water and onto her hand. "How may I help you, kind Wanyana?" he said, bowing.

"Today I have to choose a husband from three men I've never met. How can I choose wisely?" asked Wanyana, running her finger along Frog's stripes. She smiled, "Think any of them will be handsome?"

"Bulungi si 'ddya—Beauty doesn't always make a happy marriage," recited Yokana. "Handsome, rich, powerful—they might or might not be good husbands. But a man with a kind heart like yours will love you," advised Frog. He leaped onto her shoulder. "I know how we can find the right man for you." He whispered his plan in her ear.

Later that morning, Wanyana carried Frog to her front yard and set him beneath the damp, curled leaf of a young banana plant. Then she and her mother swept the hot dirt of their yard, covered it with freshly cut grass, and set out woven mats for themselves and their guests.

As they worked, Mama described meeting and marrying Wanyana's father. The stories were so real that Wanyana felt as if she were at their wedding feast—her mother crowned with bananas, her father holding a crowing rooster to announce their new marriage. Wanyana looked up at the shimmering blue of Sky God's house and smiled. Sky God's promise of the bond forever linking parent and child was true. Wanyana knew her late father's spirit was with her on this important day.

The fiery sun rose overhead while her father's sisters slowly came up the hillside. As the eldest, Aunty Nusi led the way with dignified, measured steps. Aunty Eresi, though short legged and as round as a coffee berry, had to keep stopping to avoid bumping her older sister. Aunty Nakiwala strolled behind, humming to herself.

Wanyana greeted her aunties with hugs. "When are they coming?" she asked.

"Lutaya as headman has the honor of first introduction," said Aunty Nusi, smoothing her colorful bark cloth and sitting on her mat. "He will be here soon and—"

"I can't wait for you to meet Bwoya. What a couple you two will make!" interrupted Aunty Eresi impatiently. She looked down the hillside, avoiding her elder sister's glare. "Here comes Lutaya!"

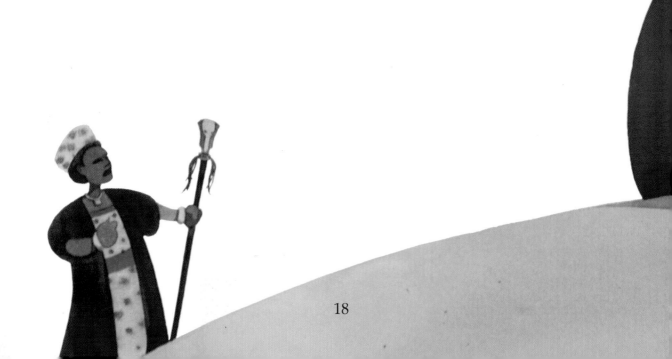

19

Wanyana took a deep breath and sat down. A muscular young man dressed in a rich, long, kkanzu robe and matching hat strode toward them.

"Wanyana, I'd like you to meet Lutaya of the Elephant Clan," said Aunty Nusi, nodding her gray head. "He is headman of Mugema village and the grandnephew of the king, our Kabaka."

Yokana Frog hopped onto Lutaya's sandal. "Blaaaat!" he croaked.

Lutaya looked down with annoyance. He shook his foot, trying to flip Frog into the grass. "Get off!" he grumbled. Yokana gripped the man's big toe, riding it like a wild donkey.

Wanyana and Aunty Nakiwala laughed behind their hands. Mama hushed them with a stern look.

Lutaya glared at Frog and flicked his foot, sending Yokana tumbling. Then he bowed to the ladies and spoke through clenched teeth. "I am Lutaya of the Elephant Clan, Chief Sali's eldest son, Chief Sempala's grandson, the Kabaka's grandnephew. Wanyana of the Otter Clan, I ask you to join our noble line." He handed a gold bracelet to Wanyana and stomped to the side of the yard to await Wanyana's decision.

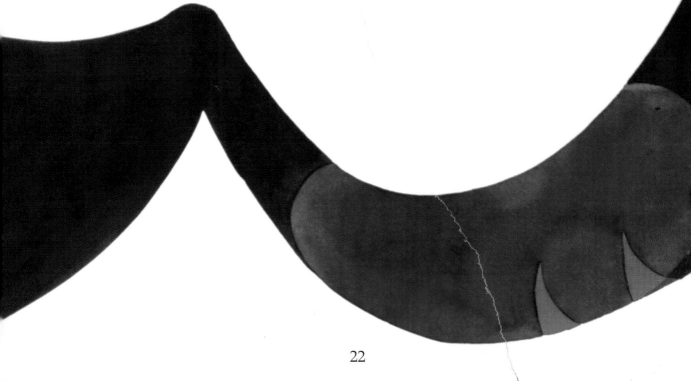

"Think carefully, my niece," advised Aunty Nusi. "He's already headman and will soon be a chief. You could live a comfortable life with a powerful man like that."

Wanyana heard her aunt, but her attention was riveted by the appearance of a very handsome man. He smoothed his gleaming robe and walked toward her, smiling with even, perfectly white teeth.

Yokana leaped in front of the handsome man, croaking, "Blaaaat!"

The young man backed up, nearly falling. "A filthy frog!" he shrieked. He grabbed a handful of grass and shooed Yokana away. "Slimy thing," he sneered, his face twisting into an ugly frown. "Did it touch my sandal? I think I see a mark." He rubbed his shoe with his thumb.

At last he straightened up and was introduced to Wanyana by Aunty Eresi. He flashed his perfect smile and said, "Wanyana, your beauty brightens the sky and makes a rainbow in my heart. Join with me, Bwoya of the Honey Bird Clan, and soar across the heavens."

As Aunty Eresi fanned herself to keep from swooning, Bwoya laid a necklace of bombo vine at Wanyana's feet. Then he joined Lutaya in waiting at the side of the yard.

The third man entered the yard with a happy bounce in his step. Aunty Nakiwala introduced him as Sempa of the Monkey Clan, a banana farmer.

Yokana hopped onto the banana farmer's sandal. "Blaaaat!" he croaked.

Sempa looked down in surprise. "I think Frog wants to be introduced too!" he laughed. He leaned down to Yokana. "Hello, Ndizaala, Little Frog."

Yokana looked at Sempa for a moment, then over at Wanyana, and then hopped away.

"I'm happy to meet you, Sempa," said Wanyana, standing. "I see you're a friend to animals. Perhaps we can be friends too."

"I am your friend, lovely Wanyana," said Sempa softly as he handed her a beautiful bark cloth. "I hope we can also be husband and wife, mother and father."

"I hope so too," said Wanyana, warmed by the happiness in Sempa's eyes and in her own heart.

As the other suitors left, Mama and the aunties nodded, silently congratulating each other on Wanyana's wise choice. They smiled at the young couple and at the helpful frog.

29

A few days later, veiled by the bark cloth Sempa had given her, Wanyana followed her mama and aunties in a procession to the pond. As the Otter Clan, the Monkey Clan, and a special member of the Clan of Frogs looked on, Wanyana took Sempa's hand and married him in a joyous ceremony.

That evening, the new couple watched the full moon rise over the pond at their banana farm. They smiled at each other and listened to Yokana's twilight song of love:

"BLAAAAT!"

PRONUNCIATION AND DEFINITION GUIDE:

Baganda (BAH´ GAN dah): People of the Bugandan empire of Uganda. They speak the Lugandan language.

bark cloth (BARK cloth): Fabric made from tree bark.

bombo (BOHM boh): A vine with white flowers.

Bwoya (BWOE yah): A Bagandan man's name.

cowrie (KOW ree): A pale, shiny shell. Long ago it was used as currency in Africa and the South Pacific.

dumbi (DOOM bee): Lugandan (the language of the Baganda) name for autumnal rains.

Eresi (EHR´ EH see): A Bagandan woman's name.

Kabaka (KAH´ BAH kah): King of Buganda.

kata-myaboosi (KAH tah-MYAH´ boh SEE): Lugandan for the hottest time of the afternoon.

Kintu (KEEN too): A legendary royal ancestor of Buganda.

kkanzu (k KAN zoo): A long robe.

Lutaya (LOO´ TAH yah): A Bagandan man's name.

ndizaala (n DEE´ ZAE lah): Lugandan name of a small frog.

Nakiwala (NAH´ kee WAH lah): A Bagandan woman's name.

Nusi (NOO see): A Bagandan woman's name.

Sempa (SEM pah): A Bagandan man's name.

Wanyana (WAHN´ YAH nah): A Bagandan woman's name.

Yokana (YOH´ KAH nah): A Bagandan man's name.